Secular
SATB (with divisions)
unaccompanied

—GABRIEL JACKSON—

How do I love thee?

to Benjamin Nicholas and Georgina Hildick-Smith on their Wedding Day

How do I love thee?

Elizabeth Barrett Browning (1806–61)

GABRIEL JACKSON

Duration: 4 mins

OXFORD UNIVERSITY PRESS, MUSIC DEPARTMENT, GREAT CLARENDON STREET, OXFORD OX2 6DP

soul can reach,___ when feel-ing out of sight For the ends___ of be-ing___ and i -

soul can___ reach,___ when feel-ing out of sight For the ends___ of be-ing___ and i -

when feel-ing out of sight For the ends___ of be-ing___ and i -

when feel-ing out of sight For the ends___ of be-ing___ and i -

- deal grace.___ I love thee to___ the le-vel of ev - 'ry day's Most

- deal grace.___ I love___ thee to___ the_ le - vel of ev - 'ry day's___Most

- deal grace.___ I love thee,

- deal grace.___ I love thee,

qui - et need,____ by sun____ and ca - a - a - a - an - dle - -light.____ I

qui - et____ need,____ by sun____ and ca - a - a - a - an - dle - -light.____ I

by sun____ and ca - a - a - a - an - dle - -light.____ I

by sun____ and ca - a - a - a - an - dle - -light.____ I

love__ thee____ free - - ly,____ as men____ strive for right;____ I

love__ thee____ free - - ly,____ as men____ strive for right;____ I

love____ thee free - ly,____ as men____ strive for right;____ I

love____ thee____ free - ly,____ as men____ strive for right;____ I

love thee purely, as they turn from praise. I

love thee purely, as they turn from praise. I

love thee purely, as they turn from praise. I

love thee purely, as they turn from praise. I

love thee with the passion put to use In my old griefs,

love thee with the passion put to use In my old griefs,

love thee with the passion put to use In my old griefs,

love thee with the passion put to use In my old griefs,

and with my child - hood's faith._____ I love thee____ with a love I seemed to

and with my child - hood's faith._____ I love thee____ with a love I seemed to

and with my child - hood's faith._____ I love thee____ with a love I seemed to

and with my child - hood's faith._____ I love thee____ with a love I seemed to

lose With my lost saints._____ I_____ love_____ thee_____ with the

lose With my lost saints._____ I_____ love_____ thee_____ with the

lose With my lost saints._____ I_____ love_____ thee_____ with the

lose With my lost saints._____ I_____ love_____ thee_____ with the

breath,_____ Smiles,_____ tears,_____ of all__ my life,___ my

life,__ of all my life;_____ and, if God choose,__ I shall_

NH240   How do I love thee?   JACKSON

Brockley, September–October 2017

ISBN 978-0-19-352908-3

9 780193 529083